Contents

How Life Continues

The aim of all living things is to reproduce more of their own kind. Most animals do this by sexual reproduction, and their young are a unique mix of their male and female parents. Sexual reproduction is successful because some of the young will combine the best elements of both their mother and father. These animals are better adapted to their environment and have the greatest chance of surviving.

The swallowtail butterfly does not stay with its young, but it ensures they have the best possible start in life. The eggs are well disguised and laid on a suitable food source, ready for when the caterpillars hatch.

Male and female animals

Most animals have two separate sexes – males and females. Males are often bigger than females, and male butterflies often have brighter colors than females. But the really important differences are in the internal organs. Males have testes that produce microscopic sperm, while the females have ovaries that produce eggs. A sperm and an egg join together in a process called fertilization to form a new animal.

Eggs or babies?

Most reptiles and birds form protective shells around their fertilized eggs and lay them as soon as possible. This means that the female is not burdened with a family of babies growing inside her. Female birds would find it impossible to fly if they gave birth to live young. On the other hand, the female has to provide each egg with a lot of food, in the form of a yolk, and this uses up a lot of her energy. Some snakes do give birth to live young, but their babies develop in a similar way, taking nourishment from the yolk of an egg. These snakes have decided that the safest nest site for their eggs is inside the mother's body.

This bear cub is a unique mix of its parents' genes. With any luck, it will have inherited the best characteristics from each. This will help it survive to produce cubs of its own – passing on the features that help it to survive in its environment.

Mammals have a different way of producing their young. Their eggs have no shells, and they grow into babies inside the female's body. The babies absorb food from their mother's blood. Carrying

Two female Atlantic spotted dolphins swim with their young. Dolphins are very sociable animals, and mothers and their young evidently enjoy each other's company.

Lions are fearsome predators, but when they are young they are in danger from other predators, such as hyenas and crocodiles. A cub's mother will guard it fiercely until it is large enough to defend itself.

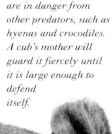

babies inside the mother's body is a good way to protect them from danger, and it also means that the mother does not have to provide a lot of food at once. Only a few babies can be born at a time, but the mammals care for their young after birth so that they have the best possible chance of surviving to become new adults.

Parental care

Many animals abandon their eggs as soon as they have laid them. Predators eat a lot of these eggs and the newly hatched young, but parents make up for it by producing huge numbers of eggs. An insect may lay hundreds or even thousands of eggs. Animals that take good care of their eggs and their young lay far fewer eggs. Some insects and spiders, and all crocodiles, make good parents, finding food for their young or coming to their defence if danger threatens.

Baby mammals feed on milk from their mother's bodies for weeks, months or even years after birth. Many babies are naked and helpless when they are born, and they are fed and kept warm in a nest or den for several weeks. Horses and other grazing animals, however, give birth to well-developed babies that can get up and walk about immediately. These animals are always on the move, and a baby must be able to keep up with its mother. Mammals that give birth to large babies have one or perhaps two babies at a time, because of the limited room in a female's body.

The new generation

Each species of animal uses a slightly different strategy to ensure that at least some of their young survive. This book examines some of those strategies. You will discover how each animal tries to ensure its genes continue, so that at least one of its offspring goes on to breed itself.

A young chimpanzee is fully at home in the treetops. With attentive care from its mother and protection from its group, this young ape should survive to have offspring of its own.

5

The Transformation of a Beetle

▲ LAYING EGGS
A cardinal beetle lays her eggs in dead wood. The hard tip of the beetle's abdomen pierces the wood to lay the eggs inside. When the eggs hatch, the log provides the larvae with a hiding place from predators. They feast on wood-eating insects until they are fully grown.

Almost all insects start their lives as eggs. They go through dramatic life changes to become fully formed adults. When beetle larvae (grubs) hatch, they look nothing like their parents. Many resemble pale worms although some have legs. They often live in different places from adult beetles and may eat quite different food.

Larvae put most of their energy into finding food, and they eat constantly. They grow bigger but do not change form. When the larva is fully grown, it changes into a pupa. Inside the pupa, the grub's body dissolves and then rebuilds in a completely different shape. It emerges from the pupa stage as an adult beetle. This amazing four-stage process of change is called complete metamorphosis. The adult beetle is now ready to look for a mate, breed and create young.

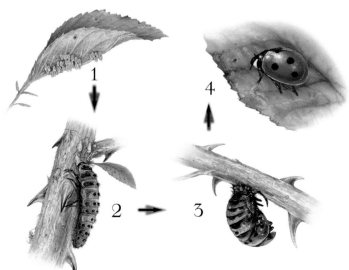

◄ ALL CHANGE
The ladybug's life cycle shows the four stages of complete metamorphosis. The adult lays eggs (1) and these hatch out into larvae or grubs (2). When fully grown, the larvae become pupae (3) before emerging as adult ladybugs (4). At each stage, the ladybug's appearance is totally different from the last, almost as if it were several animals in one.

◀ HIDDEN EGGS

These ladybug eggs have been glued onto a leaf so that they stand on end. Beetle eggs are generally round or oval, and they are usually yellow, green or black for camouflage. Eggs are usually laid in spring or summer, and most hatch between one and four weeks later. However, some eggs are laid in autumn and hatch the following spring, when there is plenty of food and conditions are warmer.

WRIGGLY LARVA ▶

A cockchafer larva has a long, fat body that is very different from the adult's rounded shape. The larva does not have the long antennae or wings of the adult either, but unlike many beetle grubs, it does have legs. It moves about by wriggling its way through the soil.

◀ UNDER COVER

When a beetle grub is fully grown, it attaches itself to a plant stem or hides underground. Then it becomes a pupa, often with a tough outer skin. Unlike the grub, the pupa doesn't feed or move much. It looks dead, but inside an amazing change is taking place. The insect's body breaks down into a thick, soup-like liquid, and is then reshaped into an adult beetle.

PERFECTLY FORMED ADULT ▶

A seven-spot ladybug struggles out of its pupa case. Like most adult beetles, it has wings, antennae and jointed legs. This ladybug's yellow wing cases will develop spots after just a few hours. Some beetles spend only a week as pupae before emerging as fully grown adults. Others pass the whole winter in the resting stage, waiting to emerge.

Caterpillar Survival

Like beetles, butterflies and moths go through a complete metamorphosis. They begin life as eggs, and hatch into caterpillars. At this stage they eat as much as possible, chomping their way through leaves, fruits and stems. They grow rapidly, shedding their skin several times as they swell. A caterpillar may grow to its full size within a month. Not all caterpillars reach the stage of becoming a chrysalis. Many are eaten by predators or killed by diseases. Caterpillars hide among vegetation and crevices in bark, often feeding at night to try to avoid danger.

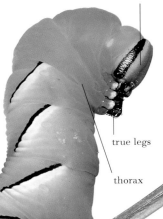

privet hawkmoth caterpillar
(*Sphinx ligustri*)

head

true legs

thorax

abdomen

this horn at the tip of the abdomen is typical of hawkmoth caterpillars

each proleg ends in a ring of hooks that are used to hold onto stems and leaves

◄ CATERPILLAR PARTS

Caterpillars have big heads with strong jaws for snipping off food. Their long, soft bodies are divided into 13 segments. The front three segments become the thorax in the adult insect and the rear segments become the abdomen.

FALSE LEGS ►

The caterpillar of an emperor gum moth has five pairs of prolegs (false legs) on its abdomen. All caterpillars have these prolegs, which help them cling on to plants. They lose the prolegs as an adult. Caterpillars also have three pairs of true legs, which become the legs of the adult.

the last pair of prolegs, called claspers, enable a caterpillar to cling very tightly to plants

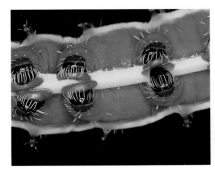

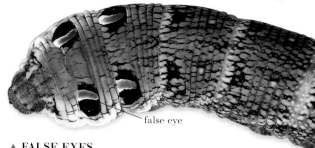

▲ BREATHING HOLES

A caterpillar does not have lungs for breathing like humans. Instead, it has tiny holes called spiracles that draw oxygen into the body tissues. There are several spiracles on each side of the caterpillar.

false eye

▲ FALSE EYES

The large eye shapes behind the head of an elephant hawkmoth caterpillar are actually false eyes for scaring predators. In fact, caterpillars can barely see at all. They possess six small eyes that can only distinguish between dark and light.

Did you know? Caterpillars can close up their spiracles and survive underwater for hours.

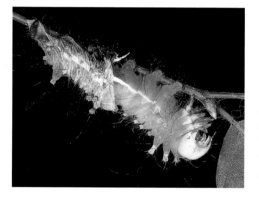

◄ CHANGING SKIN

Every week or so, the skin of a growing caterpillar grows too tight. It splits down the back to reveal a new skin underneath. At first, the new skin is soft and stretchy. As the caterpillar sheds its old skin, it swells the new one by swallowing air. It lies still for a few hours while the new large skin hardens. This skin changing process is called molting.

◄ FLY ATTACK

A puss moth caterpillar can defend itself against predators. It puffs up its front and whips its tail like a tiny dragon, before spraying a jet of poison over its foe.

SILK MAKERS ►

Peacock butterfly caterpillars live and feed in web-like tents. They spin these tents from silken thread. All caterpillars can produce this thread from a device called a spinneret under their mouth. The silk helps them to hold onto surfaces as they move.

the caterpillar's rear claspers grip a silken pad

The Birth

Once a caterpillar reaches its full size it is ready for the next stage in its metamorphosis, and it turns into a pupa or chrysalis. The caterpillars of many moths spin a silken cocoon around themselves before turning into pupae. Inside the chrysalis, the body parts of the caterpillar gradually dissolve. New features grow in their place, including a totally different head and body, and two pairs of wings. This whole process can take less than a week. When the changes are complete, almost magically, a fully formed adult emerges from the chrysalis.

1 The monarch butterfly caterpillar spins a silken pad onto a plant stem and grips it firmly with its rear claspers. It then sheds its skin to reveal the chrysalis (pupa), which clings to the silken pad with tiny hooks.

the chrysalis darkens before opening

2 The chrysalis of the monarch butterfly is plump, pale and studded with golden spots. It appears lifeless except for the occasional twitch. However, changes can sometimes be vaguely seen through the skin.

the fully formed chrysalis

3 The chrysalis grows dark and the wing pattern becomes visible just before the adult butterfly emerges. Inside, the insect pumps body fluids to its head and thorax (upper body). The chrysalis then cracks open behind the head and along the front of the wing.

# of a Butterfly

4 The butterfly swallows air to make itself swell up, which splits the chrysalis even more. The insect emerges shakily and clings tightly to the chrysalis skin.

the butterfly's wings are soft and crumpled at first

5 The newly emerged adult slowly pumps blood into the veins in its wings, which begin to straighten out. The insect hangs with its head up so that the force of gravity helps to stretch its wings. After about half an hour, the wings reach their full size.

split skin of the chrysalis

wing veins with blood pumping into them

6 The butterfly basks in the sun for an hour or two while its wings dry out and harden. After a few trial flaps of its wings, it is ready to fly away and begin life as an adult butterfly.

the bright color of the monarch butterfly warns predators that it is poisonous

monarch butterfly
(Danaus plexippus)

Spider Eggs

Female spiders are usually larger than males because they need to carry a lot of eggs inside their bodies. The eggs are usually laid a week or two after mating, although some species wait several months. Many spiders lay several batches of eggs, usually at night when they are less likely to be seen by predators. There may be from one to over 1,000 eggs per batch. Most spiders lay their eggs on a circular pad of silk, and the female then covers them with more silk to form a protective cocoon known as the egg sac.

Ananse the Spider Man

In West Africa and the Caribbean, the hero of many folk tales is Ananse. He is both a spider and a man. When things are going well Ananse is a man, but in times of danger he becomes a

spider. Ananse likes to trick the other animals and get the better of those who are much bigger than himself. He may be greedy and selfish, but he is also funny. He is a hero because he brought the gift of telling stories to people.

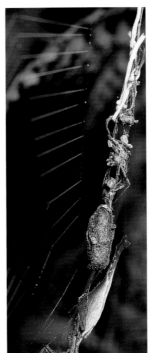

◀ **IN DISGUISE**
To hide their eggs from predators, spiders may camouflage the egg cases with plant material, insect bodies, mud or sand. This scorpion spider hangs her cocoon from a web like a string of rubbish, then poses as a dead leaf beneath them. Other species of spider hide their egg cases under stones or bark, or attach leaves around them like a purse.

▲ **SPINNING THE COCOON**
A *Nephila edulis* spider spins a cocoon. She uses special strong, loopy silk that traps a lot of air and helps to stop the eggs from drying out. Her eggs are covered with a sticky coating to attach them to the silk. The final protective blanket of yellow silk will turn green, camouflaging the cocoon.

◄ FLIMSY EGG CASE

The daddy-longlegs spider uses hardly any silk for her egg case. Just a few strands hold the eggs loosely together. Producing a large egg case uses up a lot of silk, so females with large egg cases often have shrunken bodies. The daddy-longlegs spider carries the eggs in her jaws, and so she cannot feed until the eggs have hatched.

SILK NEST ►

The woodlouse spider lays her eggs in a silken cell under the ground. She also lives in this shelter to hide from her enemies. At night, the spider emerges from its silken house to look for woodlice, which it kills with its enormous fangs.

◄ CAREFUL MOTHER

A green lynx spider protects her egg case on a cactus. She attaches the case with silk lines, like a tent's guy ropes, and attempts to drive off any enemies. If the predator persists, she cuts the silk lines and lets the cocoon swing in mid-air, balancing on top like a trapeze artist. If a female green lynx spider has to move her eggs to a safer place, she drags the case behind her with silk threads.

GUARD DUTY ►

Many female spiders carry their eggs around with them. This rusty wandering spider carries her egg case attached to her spinnerets (the organs at the back of the body that produce silk). Spiders that carry their eggs like this often sunbathe to warm them and so speed up their development.

Did you know? A female garden spider can lay over 1,000 eggs in under ten minutes.

Spiderlings

Most spider eggs hatch within a few days or weeks of being laid. The spiderlings (baby spiders) feed on egg yolk that is stored in their bodies, and they grow fast. Like insects, spiders molt to grow bigger. They shed their old skin and reveal a new, bigger skin that slowly hardens. Spiders molt several times. At first, spiderlings do not usually have any hairs, claws or color but after the first molt, the young spiders resemble tiny versions of their parents.

Most spiderlings look after themselves from the moment of hatching, but some mothers feed and guard their young until they leave the nest. Male spiders do not look after their young at all.

▲ **HATCHING**
These spiderlings are emerging from their egg case. They may have stayed inside the case for some time after hatching. Some spiders have an egg tooth to help break them out of the egg, but mother spiders may also help their young to hatch. Spiderlings from very different species look similar.

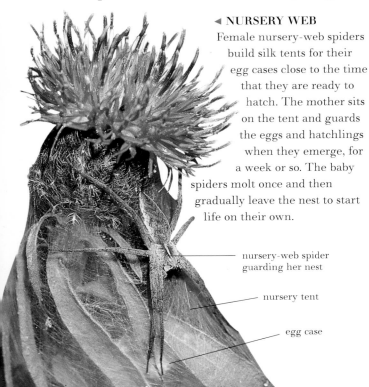

◄ **NURSERY WEB**
Female nursery-web spiders build silk tents for their egg cases close to the time that they are ready to hatch. The mother sits on the tent and guards the eggs and hatchlings when they emerge, for a week or so. The baby spiders molt once and then gradually leave the nest to start life on their own.

nursery-web spider guarding her nest

nursery tent

egg case

▲ **A SPIDER BALL**
Garden spiderlings stay together for several days after hatching. They form small gold and black balls that break apart if threatened by a predator, but re-form when the danger has passed.

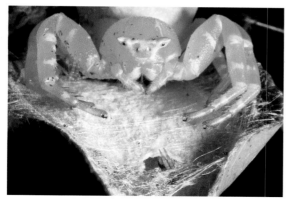

◀ BABY BODIES
A female crab spider watches over her young as they hatch. Spider eggs contain a lot of yolk, which provides a good supply of energy for the baby spiders. All spiderlings are well developed when they hatch, with the same body shape and number of legs as adults. Spiderlings, however, cannot produce silk or venom until after their first molt.

BABY CARRIER ▶
Pardosa wolf spiders carry their egg cases around with them. When the eggs are ready to hatch, the mother tears open the case and the babies climb onto her back. If the spiderlings fall off, they can find their way back by following silk lines that the mother trails behind her.

the spiderlings cling to special hairs on their mother's back for about a week

spotted wolf spider
(Pardosa amentata)

silk threads

▲ FOOD FROM MOM
The mothercare spider feeds her young on food brought up from her stomach, made of digested insects and the cells that line her gut. The babies shake her legs to beg for food. They grow faster than the young of species that have to feed themselves.

Did you know? When their mother dies, many young spiders eat her body.

▲ BALLOON FLIGHT
Many spiderlings take to the air to find new places to live or to avoid being eaten by their brothers and sisters. On a warm day with light winds, they float through the air on strands of silk they have made. This is called ballooning.

Nesting Birds of Prey

Most bird species have a different mate every year, staying together only long enough to raise their young. However, birds of prey (also known as raptors) tend to stay with one mate for life. As with all birds, courting still takes place every year to help the pair strengthen their bond and to establish their hunting territory.

Within their territory, raptors build a nest in which the female lays her eggs. Birds of prey usually nest far apart from each other because they need a large hunting area. However, some species, such as griffon vultures and lesser kestrels, nest in colonies.

The nests and nesting sites vary greatly from species to species. Nests may be an elaborate structure of branches and twigs or no more than a simple bare patch of soil on a ledge. Many pairs of raptors return to the same nest every year, adding to it until it becomes a massive structure.

▲ **FEED ME**
This female hen harrier is brooding (sitting on her eggs). Like several other raptors, male hen harriers often catch prey for their mate while she is unable to hunt for herself. Hen harriers nest on the ground, and so they need to be well camouflaged. Both the birds and the nest are hard to spot.

Bonelli's eagle
(Hieraaetus fasciatus)

◄ **SETTING UP HOME**
A Bonelli's eagle repairs her clifftop perch, keeping a careful watch over her young chick. If there are no cliffs in her territory, the female builds her nest at the top of a tall tree. The nests measure up to 6 feet across and are used year after year. Scientists have ringed this chick's leg so that its movements can be traced throughout its life.

GO AWAY! ▶

By spreading his wings to make himself look bigger, a barn owl adopts a threatening pose to protect his nest. The female has already laid several eggs, which she will incubate (sit on to keep warm) for just over a month. During this time, the male feeds her, usually with rats, mice or voles, but sometimes with insects and small birds. If food is plentiful, the pair may raise two broods a year.

◄ IN A SCRAPE

This peregrine falcon has made a nest on a cliff ledge by simply clearing a small patch of ground. This type of nest is called a scrape. Many peregrines use traditional nesting sites, where birds have made their homes for centuries. Others have adapted to life in the city, making their scrapes on the ledges of skyscrapers, office buildings or churches.

◄ FULL UP

A secretary bird comes in to land on the huge treetop nest of a flock of weaver birds in search of its own nesting site. As the tree is full, the secretary bird will have to choose another site in which to nest. It prefers low thorny trees such as acacia. Its nest is made from sticks, lined with soft grass.

secretary bird
(Sagittarius serpentarius)

▲ SECOND-HAND NEST

A disused raven's nest has been adopted by this peregrine falcon. Peregrines often lay their eggs in nests abandoned by other birds. Female peregrines usually lay 3–4 eggs, and both parents take turns to incubate them. It takes about 30 days for the eggs to hatch.

17

Young Birds of Prey

Birds of prey chicks remain in the nest for different periods, depending on the species. The chicks of small raptors, such as merlins, are nest-bound for only about eight weeks, while the offspring of larger species, such as the golden eagle, stay in their nests for more than three months. Young vultures may stay for more than five months.

As raptor chicks grow, their thick down molts to reveal proper feathers. The chicks become stronger, and start to exercise their wings by standing up and flapping them. Eventually they are ready to make their first flight. This greatest step in the life of a young bird is called fledging. It takes weeks or even months before the young birds learn all of the flying and hunting skills they need to catch prey. Until then, they are still dependent on their parents for all their food.

▲ TAKING OFF

A young kestrel launches itself into the air. It is fully grown but still has juvenile plumage. Other adults recognize the plumage and do not drive the young bird away.

▼ GROWING UP

As a tawny owl grows, its appearance changes dramatically. At four weeks old, the chick is a fluffy ball of down. Three weeks later, it is quite well feathered. At three months, the young owl is fully feathered and can fly.

4 weeks old

7 weeks old

12 weeks old

adult pygmy falcon

venile pygmy falcon
*Poliohierax
nitorquatus)

◄ BIG PYGMY

This pygmy falcon is still feeding its offspring, even though the chick is as big as its parent. In the early stages of the chick's life, the male pygmy falcon supplies all the food, while the female keeps the chick warm in the nest. Then both adults feed the fledgling, until the young bird learns to catch insects for itself. This skill can take up to two months to master.

► KESTREL COMPANY

A pair of month-old kestrels huddle together near their nest in an old farm building. They are fully feathered and almost ready to take their first flight. However, it will probably be another month before they learn to hunt.

◄ JUST PRACTICING

This young tawny owl is still unable to fly. It is flapping its wings up and down to exercise and strengthen the pectoral (chest) muscles that will enable it to fly. As the muscles get stronger, the young bird will sometimes lift off its perch. Eventually, often on a windy day, the owl will find itself flying in the air. On this first flight, it will not travel far, but within days, it will be flying as well as its parents.

tawny owl
(Strix aluco)

19

Crocodile Eggs

All crocodilians (crocodiles, alligators and gharials) lay eggs. The number of eggs laid by one female at a time ranges from about 10 to 90, depending on the species and the age of the mother. Older females lay more eggs. The length of time it takes for the eggs to hatch varies with the species and the temperature, and takes from 50 to 110 days. During this incubation period, bad weather can damage the babies developing inside the eggs. Too much rain may cause water to seep through the shells and drown the babies before they are born. Hot weather may make the inside of the egg overheat and harden the yolk, which means the baby cannot absorb the yolk and it starves to death. Another danger is that eggs laid by one female may be accidentally dug up and destroyed by another female digging a nest in the same place.

▲ EGGS FOR SALE
In many countries, people eat crocodilian eggs. They are harvested from nests and sold at local markets. This person is holding the eggs of a gharial. Each egg weighs about 4 ounces. The mother gharial lays about 40 eggs in a hole in the sand. She lays them in two tiers, separated from each other by a fairly thick layer of sand, and may spend several hours covering her nest.

▶ NEST-SITTING
The mugger crocodile of India digs a sandy pit about 10 inches deep in a river bank and lays between 10 and 50 eggs inside. She lays her eggs in layers and then covers them with a mound of twigs, leaves, soil and sand. During the 50–75 day incubation period, the female spends most of her time close to the nest. Female muggers are usually quite placid when they lay their eggs, and researchers have even been able to catch the eggs as they are laid.

► **INSIDE VIEW**

Curled tightly inside its egg, this alligator has its head and tail wrapped around its belly. Next to the developing baby is a supply of yolk, which provides it with food during incubation. Researchers have removed the top third of the shell to study the stages of growth. The baby will develop normally even though some of the shell is missing. As the eggs develop, they give off carbon dioxide gas. This reacts with moisture in the nest chamber and may make the shell thinner to let in more oxygen.

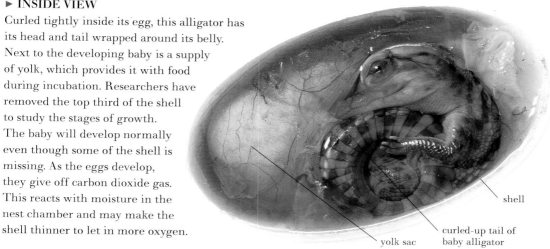

shell

curled-up tail of baby alligator

yolk sac

◄ **CRACKING EGGS**

A mother crocodile sometimes helps her eggs to hatch. When she hears the baby calling inside, she picks up the egg in her mouth. She rolls it to and fro against the roof of her mouth, pressing gently to crack the shell. The mother may have to do this for about 20 minutes before the baby breaks free from the egg.

EGGS IN THE NEST ►

All crocodilian eggs are white and oval-shaped, with hard shells like a bird's eggs. This is the nest of a saltwater crocodile, and the eggs are twice the size of chickens' eggs. It takes a female saltwater crocodile about 15 minutes to lay between 20 and 90 eggs. The eggs take up to 90 days to hatch.

Crocodiles

1 A female Nile crocodile has heard her babies calling from inside their eggs, so she knows it is time to help them escape from the nest. She scrapes away the soil and sand with her front feet and may use her teeth to cut through any roots that have grown between the eggs. Her help is very important as the soil has hardened during incubation. The hatchlings would find it difficult to dig their way up to the surface without her help.

Baby crocodilians make yelping, croaking and grunting noises from inside their eggs when it is time to hatch. The mother hears the noise and digs the eggs from the nest. The babies struggle free of their eggshells, sometimes with help from their mother. During this time, the mother is in a very aggressive mood and will attack any animal that comes near. Nile crocodile hatchlings are about 11 inches long, lively and very agile. They can give a human finger a painful nip with their sharp teeth. Their mother carries them gently in her mouth down to the water. She opens her jaws and waggles her head from side to side to wash the babies out of her mouth.

the hatchling punches a hole in its hard shell with a forward-pointing egg tooth

2 This baby Nile crocodile has just broken through its eggshell. It used a horny tip on the snout, called the egg tooth, to break through. The egg tooth is the size of a grain of sand and disappears after about a week. The egg has become thinner during the long incubation, which makes it easier for the baby to break free.

Hatching

3 Struggling out of an egg is a long, exhausting process. When the hatchlings are half out of their eggs, they sometimes take a break so they can rest before completely leaving their shells. After all the babies have hatched, the mother crushes or swallows the rotten eggs that are left.

4 Even though they are fierce predators crocodilians make caring parents. The mother Nile crocodile lowers her head into the nest and delicately picks up the hatchlings and any unhatched eggs between her sharp teeth. She gulps them into her mouth. The weight of all the babies and eggs pushes down on her tongue to form a pouch that holds up to 20 eggs and live young. Male mugger crocodiles also carry the young like this and help hatchlings to escape from their eggs.

5 A young crocodilian's belly looks fat when it hatches. This is because it contains the remains of the yolk sac, which nourished it through the incubation period. The hatchling can swim and catch its own food right away, but it continues to feed on the yolk sac for up to two weeks. In Africa, baby Nile crocodiles usually hatch just before the rainy season. The wet weather brings an abundance of food, such as insects, tadpoles and frogs for the hatchlings. Baby crocodilians are very vulnerable to predators and are guarded by their mother for at least the first few weeks of life.

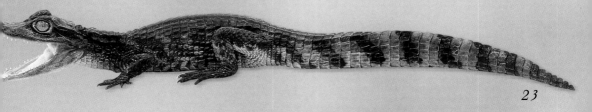

Young Crocodilians

Life is full of danger for juvenile (young) crocodilians. They are too small to defend themselves easily, despite their sharp teeth. All sorts of predators lurk in the water and on the shore, from birds of prey and pelicans, to monitor lizards, otters, tiger fish and even other crocodilians. Crocodilians lay many eggs, but not all of their young survive to hatch, and many that do, do not survive for long. Only one in ten alligators lives to the end of its first year. Juveniles often stay together in groups during the first weeks of life, yelping to each other if one gets separated. They also call loudly to the adults for help if they are in danger. By the time the juveniles are four years old, they stop making distress calls and start responding to the calls of other young individuals.

▲ INSECT DIET
A spiky-jawed Johnston's crocodile is about to snap up a dragonfly. Young crocodiles mainly eat insects. As they grow, they take larger prey, such as snails, shrimp, crabs and small fish. Their snouts gradually strengthen, so that they are able to catch bigger fish, which are the main food of this small Australian crocodile.

Did you know? 15 per cent of baby saltwater crocodiles do not survive a month.

◄ FAST FOOD
These juvenile alligators are in captivity and will grow twice as fast as they would in the wild. This is because they are fed at regular times and do not have to wait until they can catch a meal for themselves. It is also because they are kept in warm water – alligators stop feeding in cooler water. The best temperature for alligator growth is 85–90°F.

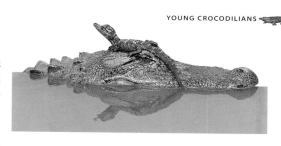

SMALL BUT SAFE ▶

Juveniles stay close to their mother for the first few weeks, resting on her back. No predator would dare to attack them there. Baby alligators are only about 10 inches long when they leave their eggs, but grow very quickly. When they have enough food to eat, male alligators grow about 12 inches a year until they are about ten years old.

▲ TOO MANY ENEMIES

The list of land predators that attack juvenile crocodilians includes big cats such as this leopard. Large wading birds, such as ground hornbills, marabou storks and herons, spear them with their sharp beaks in shallow water, while in deeper water, catfish, otters and turtles all enjoy a young crocodilian as a snack. Only about two per cent of all the eggs laid each year survive to hatch and grow into adults.

▲ CROC CRECHE

A group of crocodilian young is called a pod. Here, a Nile crocodile guards her pod as they bask in the sun. At the first sign of danger, the mother rapidly vibrates her muscles and the young immediately dive underwater. A pod may stay in the same area for as long as two years.

NOISY POD ▶

These crocodilians are caimans. A pod of juveniles, like this group, is a noisy bunch. By chirping and yelping for help, a juvenile warns its brothers and sisters that there is a predator nearby. The siblings quickly dive for shelter and hope that an adult will come to protect them. If a young Nile crocodile strays from its pod, it makes loud distress calls. Its mother, or any other female nearby, will pick up the youngster in her jaws and carry it back to the group.

Some species of snake give birth to live young, like mammals. Others lay eggs, like birds. Most egg-laying species abandon their eggs after laying them. However, some cobras and most pythons guard their eggs from predators and the weather.

Inside the egg, the baby snake feeds on the yolk. Once this has been used up the snake is fully developed and ready to hatch. All the eggs in a clutch tend to hatch at the same time.

1 As rat snakes develop inside the egg, they feed on the yolk. About eight weeks after being laid, the eggs begin to hatch.

Baby Snake Breakthroug

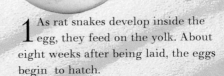

2 The baby snake is now fully developed and has become restless, twisting in its shell. It cannot get enough oxygen through the egg. The shell of a snake's egg is almost watertight, although water and gases, such as oxygen, pass in and out of it through tiny pores (holes). The baby snake cuts a slit in the shell with a sharp egg tooth on its snout. This egg tooth drops off a few hours after hatching.

3 After it has broken through the stretchy, leathery shell, the baby snake takes a rest. It pokes its nose through the slit in the egg to breathe the air and takes a first look at the strange and exciting world outside.

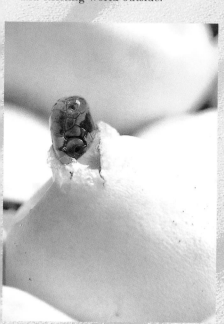

4 All the eggs in this clutch have hatched at the same time. The baby snakes will not crawl out of their shells right away. They poke their heads out of their eggs to taste the air with their forked tongues. If they are disturbed, they will slide back inside the shells where they feel safe. They may stay inside the shells for a few days.

Did you know? The mud snake lays over 100 eggs at a time.

5 Eventually, the baby snake slithers out of the egg. It may be as much as seven times longer than the egg because it was coiled up inside. It wriggles away to start a life on its own. It has to survive without any help from its parents.

rat snake
(Ptyas mucosus)

27

pope's
tree viper
(Trimeresurı
popeorum)

Snakes That Give Birth

▲ TREE BIRTH

Tree snakes often give
birth in the branches of trees.
The membrane around each baby snake sticks
to the leaves and helps stop the baby from
falling out of the branches to the ground.

▲ BIRTH PLACE

The female sand viper chooses a quiet, remote
spot to give birth to her young. Snakes usually
give birth in a hidden place, where the young
are safe from enemies.

Did you know? An anaconda may have 100 babies at a time.

Instead of laying eggs, some snakes
give birth to fully developed, live
young. Snakes that do this include
boas, rattlesnakes and adders. The
young develop in an egg inside the
mother's body. The surface of the
egg is a thin protective membrane
instead of a shell. The baby snake gets
its food from yolk inside the egg.
Anything from six to 50 babies are
born at a time, depending on the
species. The baby snakes are still inside
their membranes when they are born.

BABY BAGS ▶

These red-tailed boas
have just been born. They are
still inside their tough
membranes, which are made
of a thin, see-through material,
like the one inside the shell
of a hen's egg.

28

BREAKING FREE ▶

A baby rainbow boa has just pushed its head through the membrane that surrounds it. Snakes have to break free on their own. Each baby has an egg tooth to cut a slit in the membrane so that it can wriggle out. They usually do this a few seconds after birth.

◀ NEW BABY

A red-tailed boa has broken free of its membrane, the remains of which can be seen around the body. Some newborn snakes crawl off straight away, while others stay with their mother for a few days.

◀ COLOR CHANGE

Emerald tree boas are bright red when they are born. It takes a year for them to turn the vivid green of their parents.

Did you know? Baby boa constrictors grow from 20 inches to 40 inches in their first year.

Egg-laying Sharks

Sharks are fish, not mammals, and so their young do not suckle from their mother or need to breathe air. Sharks bring their young into the world in two ways. In most species, eggs grow into baby sharks inside the mother's body. The mother gives birth to active young called pups. In other species, the female shark lays eggs, each enclosed in a tough case or capsule. Young catsharks grow in cases like this. Each mating season, catsharks lay up to 20 cases and attach them to seaweed. A single pup develops inside each capsule. Catsharks do not guard or look after their egg cases in any way. Instead, they rely on the tough, leathery case to protect the pup inside.

▲ EGG WITH A TWIST
The egg case of a horn shark has a spiral-shaped ridge. The mother shark uses her mouth like a screwdriver to twist the case around and attach it firmly to gaps in rocks.

▲ TIME TO LEAVE
When it is ready to leave its egg, the baby horn shark uses special scales on its snout and fins to cut its way out of the tough egg case. The dorsal fins on its back have tough spines that protect it from the moment it emerges.

Mermaid's Purses
The mermaid is a mythical undersea creature with a woman's body and a fish's tail. In legends, mermaids lured men to their deaths with beautiful songs. Catshark egg cases, which are sometimes washed up on beaches, look like pouches, and are often called mermaid's purses.

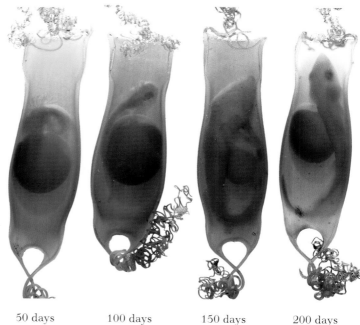

50 days   100 days   150 days   200 days

◄ ▲ IN THE SAC

In the earliest stages of development, the catshark pup is tiny, about the size of a pea. It is attached to a huge, yellow yolk sac from which it takes its food. Inside the egg case, the growing pup makes swimming movements, which keep the egg fluids and the supply of oxygen fresh. After nine months, the catshark pup breaks free of the case.

► SWELL SHARK

The length of time it takes the swell shark pup to grow and hatch from its case depends on the temperature of the sea water around it. In warm water, it can take just seven months. In cold water, it might take ten months. The pup has special skin teeth to tear its capsule open.

31

The Birth of a

1 By pumping sea water over her gills, a pregnant lemon shark can breathe while resting on the seabed. She gives birth on the sandy lagoon floor to the pups that have developed inside her for a year.

A year after mating, pregnant lemon sharks arrive at Bimini Island, off the coast of Miami, in the Atlantic Ocean. Here, they give birth to their pups in a shallow lagoon where males do not enter. An adult male is quite likely to eat a smaller shark, even one of its own kind. In many species of shark, pregnant females leave the males and swim to safer nursery areas to give birth. Some scientists even believe that females lose their appetite at pupping time, to avoid eating their own young. After birth, the lemon shark pups live on their own.

2 Baby lemon sharks are born tail first. Female sharks give birth to 5–17 pups at one time. Each pup is about 24 inches long. After her pups are born, a female lemon shark will not be able to mate again right away. Instead, she will rest for a year.

Lemon Shark Pup

3 A lemon shark gives birth to her pups in the shallows. The pups are still attached to the umbilical cord when born, but a sharp tug soon frees them. The small remora fish that follow the shark everywhere will feast on the discarded umbilical cord.

4 After birth, a baby lemon shark makes for safety in the shallow, muddy waters at the edge of the lagoon. It spends the first few years of its life among the tangled roots of the mangrove trees that grow there. The pup feeds on small fish, worms and shellfish. It must be wary of sharks larger than itself, which may try to eat it.

5 To avoid being eaten, young lemon sharks gather with others of the same size. Each group patrols its own section of the lagoon at Bimini. This young lemon shark is about one year old. When it is seven or eight, it will leave the safety of the lagoon and head for the open reefs outside.

The Birth

1 Some mares lie on their side during foaling, while others remain standing. The foal emerges head first, with its forelegs extended. It only takes a few minutes for it to be born. At first, it is still enclosed in the membrane in which it developed in the womb, but it soon breaks free by shaking itself or standing up.

2 The placenta, through which the foal received nutrients when it was still in the womb, comes out immediately after the birth. The mother might chew on this, but she does not eat it.

3 The mother licks the newborn foal all over to establish her bond with the baby. From now on, she will be able to recognize her foal from all others. It will take about a week, however, for the foal to know its mother.

Horses belong to the large group of animals called mammals. Like almost all mammals, the babies grow inside their mother, taking their nourishment from her rather than the yolk of an egg. This means the young can be born fairly well developed. All mammals feed their young on milk.

In the wild, horses, zebras and asses give birth when there is plenty of food and water around and weather is not too extreme. The breeding season is usually brief so that all the foals in one area will be born at about the same time. They have a greater chance of survival from predators if all of the foals are the same age, rather than being born in ones or twos throughout the year.

# of a Baby Horse

4 The newborn foal struggles to its feet. It will stand up within ten minutes of birth, and will soon be able to canter. The foal's first few days of life are taken up with feeding, practicing using its legs and napping. Feeds last for a few minutes each, and a rest may be between 20 minutes and one hour long.

5 The mother is very aggressive at this time. She chases other horses away and may even bite them. This ensures that the foal will imprint on her (recognize her as its source of food and protection) rather than any other animal in the herd. After about a week, the mare calms down, and the foal is allowed to meet with others of its own kind.

LOOKING FOR FOOD
Instinct tells this plains zebra foal that its mother's teats are found between the legs and the belly, but it might search between the forelegs before finding the right spot.

TWO YEARS UNTIL INDEPENDENCE
This wild ass foal will stay with its mother for two years. Asses usually foal every two years, but horses and zebras sometimes have one foal a year, if conditions are good.

Elephant Calves

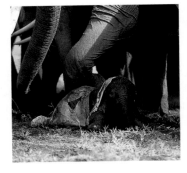

▲ BIRTH TIME
A baby elephant emerges from its mother in a protective membrane called a birth sac. The other females in the group sniff the newcomer and softly touch it all over, while rumbling with excitement.

Female elephants live in family groups with their mothers, sisters, daughters and their offspring. Like horses, females often have babies at about the same time, at the time of year that food is most plentiful.

An elephant's pregnancy lasts for nearly two years, and females only have one calf every four to six years. A female elephant may have her first calf at the age of 10 and her last when she is 50. She has between five and 12 babies in a lifetime.

Young elephant calves are highly vulnerable, and about a third do not survive to reach adulthood. Some are taken by predators, such as crocodiles, lions and tigers. Others drown or are crushed by falling trees. All the elephants in the group try to keep the calves safe.

a baby elephant practices using its trunk

▲ TRUNK TRICKS
Baby elephants are curious and inquisitive. They want to touch and feel everything with their trunk. At first, they cannot control their long, wobbly nose. They trip over it or suck on it — just as human babies suck their thumbs. It takes them months of practice to learn how to use their trunks.

▶ THIRSTY CHILD
A calf sucks milk from its mother's breasts with its mouth. The milk is thin and watery, but very nourishing. Babies put on weight at a rate of 25—45 pounds per month.

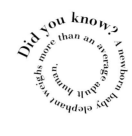

◄ LEARNING FAST

A young elephant has to master the technique of giving itself a dust bath. It must also learn to pick up and carry things with its trunk, drink, feed and have a mudbath. If a young elephant cannot reach water, the mother sucks up water in her trunk and squirts it down her baby's throat.

Did you know? A newborn baby elephant weighs more than an average adult human.

GUIDING TRUNK ►

At first, a baby elephant sticks close to its mother night and day. It is always within reach of a comforting touch from her strong, guiding trunk. The mother encourages her baby, helps it to keep up with other members of the herd and often pulls it back if it starts to stray. Baby elephants will die quickly if they are left on their own.

▲ PROPER FOOD

After a few months, calves begin to eat plants. A calf may put its trunk into its mother's mouth to taste her food and learn which plants are edible.

▲ HELPFUL RELATIVES

The survival of both mothers and calves depends greatly on the support of the family group. Each member of the group takes part in bringing up the babies. This helps the mother, and allows young female elephants to learn how to care for calves.

Caring Elephant Families

A baby elephant is brought up by its family in a fun-loving, easy-going and caring environment. At first, a calf spends a lot of time with its mother, but as it grows older and stronger, it begins to explore and make friends with other calves. Young elephants spend a lot of time playing together. They can do this because they feed on their mother's milk and so they do not have to spend all day finding food. Gradually, the calf learns all the skills it will need as an adult.

▲ **BROTHERS AND SISTERS**
A female elephant may have a calf every five years, but elephants do not become adults until they are about ten years old. Usually, just when the first calf can feed itself, another one arrives. The older calf still spends a lot of time with its mother.

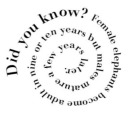

Did you know? Female elephants become adult in nine or ten years but males mature a few years later.

◄ **MOTHER'S MILK**
A calf drinks its mother's milk until it is between four and six years old. By then, the mother usually needs her milk for the next baby. Even so, calves as old as eight have been known to push a younger brother or sister out of the way to steal a drink.

◀ PLAYTIME

A growing elephant learns a lot simply by playing. Male elephants push and shove each other to test their strength. Females play games with lots of chasing, like tag. Both males and females like to mess about in mud, dust and water.

▲ PROTECTING THE YOUNG

All the adults in a family are protective of the young. They shade calves from the sun and stand guard over them while they sleep. Small calves are vulnerable to attack from many other animals, including poisonous snakes.

Ganesh

In the Hindu religion of India, Ganesh is the elephant-headed god of wisdom and the remover of obstacles. Ganesh's father, the god Siva, is said to have cut off Ganesh's head. His mother, the goddess Parvati, was so angry that she forced Siva to give her son a new head. This new head turned out to be that of an elephant. Hindus seek good luck from Ganesh before the start of important business.

◀ LOTS OF MOTHERS

Allomothers are female elephants in the group that take a special interest in the upbringing of calves. They wake up the calf when it is time to travel, help it if it gets stuck in mud and protect it from danger.

▲ NEWBORN GORILLA
This day-old gorilla is tiny and helpless as it clings to its mother's fur. Its wrinkled face is a pinkish color and its big ears stick out. Soon after birth, the baby's brown eyes open and peer curiously at its surroundings. Despite its long, skinny arms and legs, the baby gorilla is quite strong.

Did you know? A gorilla usually gives birth in less than an hour.

Baby Great Apes

The great apes — gorillas, orangutans, chimpanzees, gibbons and bonobos — usually have one baby at a time and spend many years looking after their young, just as humans do. Most apes are pregnant for eight or nine months, although baby gibbons are born after seven or eight months.

Baby apes are much smaller than human babies and weigh only about half as much. This means that giving birth is easier for an ape than for a human mother. Both labor and birth are fairly swift and trouble-free. Newborn apes are almost helpless, but they have a very strong grip so they can cling to their mother's hair. She feeds them on her milk and may carry them around for four or five years as they gradually grow up and become more independent.

◄ MILK FROM MOM
A newborn baby gorilla depends on its mother's milk for nourishment. After six to eight months, it gradually begins to try different bits of plant food, but it continues to drink its mother's milk for at least two years.

chimpanzees
(Pan troglodytes)

gorillas
(Gorilla gorilla)

PIGGY-BACK ▶

Riding piggy-back on its mother's broad back, a baby gorilla watches the other gorillas and looks around its habitat as the group travels from place to place. This is the safest place for the young gorilla until it is strong enough to walk by itself.

▲ HITCHING A RIDE

Very young chimpanzees are carried underneath their mother, clinging on to her fur with their tiny fists. By the age of five to six months, a baby chimp starts to ride on its mother's back. It is alert, looking around and touching things.

◀ GOOD PARENTS

Baby gibbons depend on their mothers for warmth and milk. Gibbon fathers groom their babies and play with them. Siamang gibbon fathers look after their youngsters during the day.

▲ CHIMP CHILDHOOD

The bond between a mother chimpanzee and her baby is strong and lasts throughout their lives. A young chimp is completely dependent on its mother for the first five years. It stays close to its mother so that she can see and hear it.

41

The Life of a

MOTHER LOVE

There is a very strong bond between a mother orangutan and her baby. When she is not moving through the trees or feeding, the mother may groom her baby or suckle it, although she doesn't often play with it. A baby orangutan may scream and throw a tantrum to get its mother's attention.

Young orangutans live a different life from gorilla and chimpanzee babies. Instead of being brought up in a group, the orangutan's world is almost entirely filled by its mother. Most orangutans live alone, but following the birth of a baby, a mother becomes even more shy than usual. She tries to avoid other orangutans in order to protect her baby.

For the first year of its life, a baby orangutan is entirely dependent on its mother, and she cares for it without any help. A young orangutan stays with its mother for seven to nine years, gradually learning what to eat, where to find food, how to climb and swing through the trees safely, and how to make a nest to sleep in.

MOTHER'S MILK

For the first year of its life, a baby orangutan drinks its mother's milk and clings to her chest or back. After a year, it starts to eat solid food but it continues to suck for another three to five years. Like most baby mammals, orangutans are keen to take their mother's milk for as long as possible.

Young Orangutan

NEST-BUILDING
Orangutans sleep in nests made with leafy branches. During their second year, young orangutans experiment with making their own nests.

PLAYTIME
Although they are usually solitary, on the rare occasions young orangutans meet they wrestle and play together in the forest. They may get so carried away that they do not notice when their mother leaves. Then they have to hurry after her, screaming angrily as they go.

SOLID FOOD
To start her baby on solid food, a mother orangutan partly chews up bits of food and then presses them into the baby's mouth. Young orangutans eagerly take the solid food.

A NEW BABY
When an orangutan is between five and eight years old, its mother may give birth again. The new baby takes most of the mother's attention, and the young orangutan becomes more independent. Even so, it may stay with its mother for a year or more after the new baby is born.

43

Great Ape Childhood

Apes spend a long time growing up. As well as learning how to move, feed and defend themselves, they have to know how to behave with others of their own kind. This is especially important for chimpanzees and gorillas because they live in large groups. Young apes do not become independent of their mothers until they are aged about eight. Female orangutans and gorillas will not have babies of their own until they are about ten years old, and female chimps not until they are 14. Male orangutans and gorillas will not have offspring until they are about 15 years of age. When they are grown up, orangutans and gibbons leave their parents to start a life of their own. Most gorillas and female chimps also leave the group they were born into.

orangutans
(*Pongo pygmaeus*)

▲ MOTHER AND BABY

Female orangutans spend most of their adult lives caring for their offspring. An orangutan may have only four young in her lifetime.

▲ APE EXPLORER

Young chimps love to explore, moving farther away from their mothers as they test their climbing skills. At the first sign of danger, though, they run back to their mothers.

44

▲ SPEEDY GORILLAS

Baby gorillas develop through the same stages of movement as human babies, only much faster. They can crawl at nine weeks of age and walk by nine months – an age when most human babies have only just started to crawl.

▲ FOOD FROM MOTHER

A chimpanzee watches its mother and other chimps to find out what is good to eat. Young chimps chew the other end of whatever food their mother is eating.

◄ PLAYING THE GAME

Little chimps have a lot of free time, which they spend at play. Young females spend much of their time playing with the babies in their group. Through playing, the chimps learn the rules of chimpanzee society.

chimpanzee
(Pan troglodytes)

Did you know? Young gorillas have a white tuft on their rear to help their mothers find them.

AT PLAY ►

Young gorillas wrestle, chase, playfight and climb and slide all over the adults. This helps them to test their strength, build up their muscles and learn how to get along with other gorillas.

Inside a Bear Den

Bear cubs are born naked and helpless at the harshest time of year. They are absolutely tiny compared to the size of an adult bear and need to be protected from the cold weather as well as from predators. A den, hidden away from the outside world, makes a perfect home. The den can be in a cave, a hollow tree or a self-made hollow.

The female bear does not leave the den for the first few months. She does not hunt, but relies on her fat reserves to survive. Producing enough milk to nourish her cubs takes a lot of energy, and a mother bear is only able to feed them if she has eaten enough food in the months before.

▲ **BLIND AND HELPLESS**
Ten-day-old brown bear cubs nestle into their mother's fur for warmth. With their eyes and ears tightly closed shut, they are totally dependent on her. The cubs remain in the den until May or June when they are about four months old.

Did you know? Polar bear cubs are no bigger than guinea pigs when they are born.

◄ **POLAR TWINS**
A polar bear mother tends her two young. The family leaves its den between late February and April depending on where it lives. The farther north the bears are, the later in the year they emerge.

polar bear
(Ursus maritimus)

▲ TRIPLE TROUBLE

This American black bear has given birth to three healthy cubs. Females may have up to four cubs at one time. Newborn black bear cubs are about the size of a rat, but they grow quickly. They leave the den in April or May.

▲ PANDA BABY

At Wolong breeding station in Sichuan, China, a baby giant panda is put in a box to be weighed. Giant pandas give birth to one or two cubs in a cave or tree hollow. If twins are born, the mother often rears only one, leaving the other to die.

◄ MOTHER'S MILK

Three-month-old polar bear cubs feed on their mother's milk. Unlike most bear cubs, polar bears are born covered with fine hair to help keep them warm in the bitter Arctic weather.

IN THE DEN ►

Newborn American black bears weigh less than 12 ounces, which is about the same as a can of soda pop. Their small size and lack of fur makes them vulnerable to the cold. The mother cleans and dries the cubs, then cuddles them close. The den is lined with branches, leaves, and grasses to make a warm blanket. The mother spends a lot of time grooming her cubs and keeps the den scrupulously clean by eating their droppings.

Snow Den

From late October, a pregnant female polar bear digs a snow den. Usually it is some distance from the sea, on a slope facing south. This means the den's entrance and exit hole faces towards the sun, which is low on the horizon in early spring. The sun's rays help to warm the den.

The mother bear gives birth during the harshest part of winter, when permanent night covers the Arctic. The den is kept warm and snug with heat from her body. A tunnel to the nursery chamber slopes upwards so that warm air rises and collects in the chamber, which can be 40°F warmer than outside.

1 A bank of snow makes an ideal site for a polar bear's winter den. The pregnant female bear digs about 15 feet into the south side of the snowdrift. The wind in the Arctic blows mainly from the north, so the snow piles up on the other side.

2 This picture is an artist's impression of the inside of a polar bear's den. The cubs are about three months old and they are almost ready to leave their snow home for the first time. Polar bear cubs are born between late November and early January, but don't leave the den until the spring.

3 The female polar bear emerges from her winter home. She drives two holes through the walls of the den and helps the cubs make their first journey outside. The family remains near the den site for a few days so the cubs become used to the cold.

for Polar Bears

4 Sitting upright in a snow hollow, a female polar bear nurses her cubs. She differs from other female bears in that she has four working nipples rather than six. Her cubs stay with her for three years, which is a year longer than the average for bears. During the years they spend with her, the cubs will learn how to survive in the cold Arctic conditions and also how to hunt seals for food.

5 The cubs play outside in the snow during the short days, and shelter in the den at night and during storms. Soon the family leaves the den altogether and heads towards the sea where the mother can hunt and feed.

6 The cubs' first journey is often a long one. They may have to walk up to 14 miles to reach the sea ice where they will see their first seal hunt. The mother takes great care to avoid danger on the journey. She looks out for adult male polar bears who might try to kill her cubs.

Bear Cubs

Young bears spend their first 18 months to three years with their mother. If she dies, they may be adopted by another mother with cubs the same age. The cubs learn everything from their mother. She teaches them how to recognize the best food and where and when to find it. The cubs must also learn how to escape danger and how to find a winter den or shelter in a storm. Without this schooling, the young bears would not survive. Mothers and cubs communicate by calling, particularly if they become separated from each other.

During their development, cubs must keep out of the way of large male bears who might attack and kill them.

▲ SAFE IN THE BRANCHES

Black bear cubs instinctively know that they should head for the nearest tree when danger threatens. It is easier for a mother to defend a single tree than a scattered family.

▼ FEEDING TIME

A mother brown bear suckles her twins. Her milk is thick and rich in fats and proteins, but low in sugars. It has three times the energy content of human or cow milk. The milk also contains antibodies, which help protect the cubs from disease.

brown bear
(Ursus arctos)

◄ LEAVING THE FAMILY

Young bears on their own, such as this brown bear, often become thin and scrawny. Despite being taught by their mothers where and how to feed, they are not always successful. At popular feeding sites, such as fishing points, they may be chased off by larger bears. When the time comes for young bears to look after themselves, the mother either chases them away or is simply not there when they return to look for her.

A LONG APPRENTICESHIP ►

Polar bear cubs are cared for by their mother for much longer than other bear cubs. They need to master the many different hunting strategies used by their mother to catch seals. These are not something that the cubs know instinctively, but skills that they must learn.

polar bear
(Ursus maritimus)

Did you know? Giant panda cubs are the first bears to leave their mother at 18 months old.

◄ FAMILY TRAGEDY

This polar bear cub is the victim in a tragic tug-of-war. A male bear has attacked the cub and its mother is trying to save it. Female bears fight ferociously to protect their young, but are often unsuccessful against the larger males. About 70 per cent of polar bear cubs do not live to their first birthday. Attacks by adult male bears, starvation, disease and the cold are the usual causes of death.

51

Big Cat Babies

The cubs (babies) of a big cat are usually born with spotted fur and closed eyes. They are completely helpless. The mother cat looks after them on her own with no help from the father. She gives birth in a safe place called a den. For the first few days after birth, she stays very close to her cubs so that they can feed on her milk. She keeps them warm and cleans the cubs by licking them all over. The cubs grow quickly. They can crawl even before their eyes open, and they soon learn to hiss to defend themselves.

▲ SNOW CUB

Snow leopard cubs have white fur with dark spots, and they are always born in the spring. The cubs begin to follow their mothers around when they are about three months old. By winter, they will be almost grown up.

MOTHERLY LOVE ▶

Tiger cubs are capable killers by the time they are 11 months old. They stay with their mothers, however, until they are two or even three years of age. A female tiger does all she can to protect her young, but often at least half of the litter dies. Predators may kill the cubs, or sometimes they starve to death if the mother cannot catch enough food.

cheetah cub
(*Acinonyx jubatus*)

IN DISGUISE ▶

A cheetah cub is covered in long, woolly fur. This makes it resemble the African honey badger, a very fierce animal, which may help to discourage predators. The mother cheetah does not raise her cubs in a den, but moves them around every few days.

▲ BRINGING UP BABY

Female pumas give birth to up to six kittens at a time. The mother has several pairs of teats for the kittens to suckle from. Each baby has its own teat and will use no other. They will take their mother's milk for at least three months, and from about six weeks they will also eat meat.

▲ ON GUARD

Two lionesses guard the entrance to their den. Lions are social cats and share the responsibility of keeping guard. Dens are kept very clean so that there are no smells to attract predators.

▲ MOVING TO SAFETY

If at any time a mother cat thinks her cubs are in danger, she will move them to a new den. She carries the cubs one by one, gently grasping the loose skin at their necks between her teeth.

53

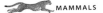

Cubs Growing Up

Young cubs have to learn all about life as an adult big cat so that they can eventually look after themselves. Their mother teaches them as much as she can, and the rest they learn through play. As cubs play, they learn how to judge distances and when to strike to kill prey quickly, without getting injured or killed themselves. The exact games cubs play vary from one species of cat to another, because each has different hunting techniques to learn. Cheetahs, for instance, playfight using their paws to knock each other over. Lions play by biting each other's throats.

Mothers and cubs generally use very high-pitched sounds to communicate, but if the mother senses danger, she growls at her cubs to tell them to hide.

▲ **PRACTICE MAKES PERFECT**
These cheetah cubs are learning to kill a Thomson's gazelle. When the cubs are about 12 weeks old, a mother cheetah brings back live injured prey for them to kill. They instinctively know how to do so, but need practice to get it right.

▼ **FOLLOW MY LEADER**
Curious cheetah cubs watch an object intently, safe beside their mother. At about six weeks, the cubs start to go on hunting trips with her. They are able to keep up by following her white-tipped tail through the tall grass.

cheetah
(*Acinonyx jubatus*)

THE CLASSROOM ▶

These lion cubs lounge on a fallen tree. From here they
watch the adults hunt, as if in a big, open-
air classroom. Females stay in the same
pride (group) all their lives, but
young males will
leave at about
three years
old.

lion cubs
(Panthera leo)

◀ WHAT IS IT?

Three young lions sniff at the
shell of a tortoise. Cubs learn
to be cautious when dealing
with unfamiliar objects. First,
the object is tapped with a
paw, before being explored
further with the nose. Cubs'
milk teeth are replaced with
permanent canine teeth at
about two years old. Not
until then can they begin to
hunt and kill big animals.

TAIL TOY ▶

A mother leopard's tail is a
good thing for her cub to
learn to pounce on. She
twitches it so that the cub
can develop accurate timing
and coordination. As the cub
grows, it practises on rodents
and then bigger animals
until it can hunt for itself.

Once they leave their
mothers, female cubs usually
establish a territory close by,
while males go farther away.

55

Newborn Wolves

Most wolf packs have between 8 and 24 members. Only the leaders will mate and have cubs, but every pack member then helps to bring up the cubs.

Newborn wolves are helpless. They cannot hear, their eyes are tightly closed and their legs are too weak to allow them to stand. The cubs squirm around and huddle close to their mother for warmth. Like all mammals, their first food is their mother's rich milk.

After one or two weeks, the cubs' eyes open and they begin to take notice of their surroundings. They take their first wobbly steps and scramble over each other in the den. At about five weeks, the cubs start to take solid food as well as milk. Half-chewed meat, stored in the stomach of an adult wolf, is brought to the den and regurgitated (coughed up) when the cubs beg for food.

▲ AT THE DEN

Wolf cubs take a first look at the big world outside their den. For nearly eight weeks, their only experience has been the burrow — a 13-foot-long tunnel dug in soft earth with room for an adult wolf to creep along. The cubs sleep in a cozy chamber at the end.

Did you know? The mother of the wolf cubs sleeps in a hollow near the entrance of the den.

NURSING MOTHER ▶

Like bears, most wolves are born in a den, and the female stays with her cubs for the first few weeks. A wolf mother, however, does not have to rely on fat reserves as bears do. Her mate, and the rest of the pack, bring food so that she does not have to go hunting. She needs large quantities of food to produce enough milk for her cubs.

▼ CUBS IN DANGER

These wolf cubs are six or seven weeks old. Not all cubs are born in a den. Some are born in a sheltered hollow, or in a nest flattened in long grass. There are many dangers for cubs in the open, including being snatched by predators such as bears and eagles. Many do not survive to adulthood.

gray wolf cubs
(Canis lupus)

Romulus and Remus

According to ancient Roman legend, Romulus and Remus were twin brothers who were abandoned as babies on a remote hillside. A she-wolf found them and brought them up, feeding them on her milk. Both brothers survived, and Romulus went on to found the city of Rome.

▲ HUNGRY PUPPIES

An African hunting dog suckles her pups. They suck milk from two sets of nipples on her underside. Female hunting dogs often have more nipples than other canids, because they have the biggest litters and therefore the most mouths to feed. As the pups' sharp teeth begin to hurt, she will wean them onto meat.

▲ RARE CUBS

In the mountains of Ethiopia, a female Simien wolf guards her litter of five cubs. Simien wolves are much rarer than other wolves. These cubs look healthy, so have a good chance of surviving long enough to breed as adults.

Older Wolf Cubs

At eight weeks old, wolf cubs are very lively. Their snouts have grown longer, their ears stand up and they look much more like adult wolves. They bound about on long, strong legs. Now weaned off milk, they live on a diet of meat brought by the adults. As they leave the safety of the den, the other pack members gather round and take great interest in the cubs. The cubs' new playground is the rendezvous, the safe place at the heart of wolf-pack territory where the adults gather. This is usually a sheltered, grassy spot near a stream where the cubs can drink. Here they develop their hunting skills by pouncing on mice and insects. As they playfight, they establish a ranking order that mirrors the social order in the pack.

▲ CARRIED AWAY

A wolf carries a cub to safety by seizing the loose skin at the scruff of its neck in its teeth. This adult is most likely the cub's mother or father, but it may be another member of the pack. All the adult wolves are very tolerant of the youngsters to begin with. Later, as the cubs grow up, they may be punished with a well-placed nip if they are naughty.

Did you know? Father wolves make squeaking noises to call their cubs.

SHARING A MEAL ▶

A young African hunting dog begs for food by whining, wagging its tail and licking the adult's mouth. The adult responds by arching its back and regurgitating a meal of half-digested meat from its stomach. The pups grow quickly on this diet. At the age of four months, they are strong enough to keep up with the pack when it goes hunting.

▼ PRACTICE MAKES PERFECT

Two Arctic fox cubs practice their hunting skills by pouncing on one another. Young cubs playfight to establish a ranking order. By the age of 12 weeks, one cub has managed to dominate the others. He or she may go on to become leader of a new pack.

Wolfchild

Rudyard Kipling's Jungle Book, *which was published in 1894, is set in India. The book tells the story of Mowgli, a young boy who is abandoned and brought up by wolves in the jungle. When Mowgli becomes a man he fights his archenemy, the tiger Shere Khan. Kipling's tale was inspired by many true-life accounts of wolf-children who grew up in the wild in India during the 1800s.*

▲ YOUTHFUL CURIOSITY

Young maned wolves investigate their surroundings. Females usually bear three cubs at most. Newborn young have grey-brown fur, short legs and snouts. Later they develop long legs and handsome red fur.

ALMOST GROWN ▶

These two young wolves are almost full grown. Cubs can feed themselves at about ten months, but remain with the pack to learn hunting skills. At about two or three years old, many are turned out. They wander alone or with brothers or sisters until they find mates and start new packs.

Baby Whales

BIRTH DAY
A bottlenose dolphin gives birth. The baby i[s] born tail-first. This birth is taking place near the bottom of an aquarium. In the wild, birth takes place close to the surface so the bab[y] can surface quick[ly] and start breathi[ng]

Although they live in the sea, whales are mammals, which means that they breathe air and the mother feeds her young with milk. Many whales are enormous, and so are their babies. A newborn blue whale can weigh up to 2½ tons, which is twice as much as a family car.

The first thing a newborn whale must do is to take a breath. Its mother and perhaps another whale may help it up to the surface. After that, the calf can breathe and swim unaided. Baby whales feed on their mother's milk for several months until they learn to take solid food such as fish. Mother and calf may spend most of the time alone, or join nursery schools with other mothers and calves.

SUCKLING
A beluga mother suckles her young. Her fatty milk is very nutritious, and the calf grows rapidly. It will drink milk for up to two years. At birth the calf's body is dark grey, but it slowly lightens as the calf matures.

and Dolphins

Did you know? Blue whales are born in tropical waters, but nine months later they are thousands of miles away in cold polar waters.

AT PLAY

A young Atlantic spotted dolphin and its mother play together, twisting, turning, rolling and touching each other with their flippers. During play, the young dolphin learns the skills it will need later in life when it has to fend for itself. The youngster is darker than its mother and has no spots. These do not start to appear until it is about a year old.

TOGETHERNESS

A humpback whale calf sticks closely to its mother as she swims slowly in Hawaiian waters. The slipstream (water flow, created by the mother's motion) helps pull it along. For the first few months of its life, the calf will not stray far from its mother's side.

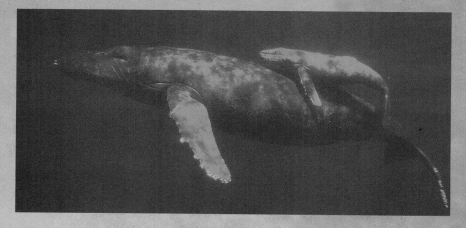

Glossary

abdomen
The rear section of an animal's body. It holds the reproductive organs and part of the digestive system.

antennae (singular: antenna)
The "feelers" on top of an insect's head, which are used for smelling, touching and tasting.

ballooning
Floating away on strands of silk blown by the wind.

bird of prey
A bird, such as an eagle, that catches and kills its prey with powerful hooked claws called talons.

brood
(1) The number of babies a mother has at one time.
(2) When a bird sits on its eggs to incubate them.

camouflage
The colors or patterns that allow an animal to blend in with its surroundings.

canid
A member of the dog family. The group includes wolves, foxes and African hunting dogs.

canine teeth
Sharp, pointed teeth that grip prey and pierce the skin.

caterpillar
The second, larval stage in the life of a butterfly or moth, after it has hatched from the egg. A caterpillar has a long tube-like body with 13 segments and many legs. It has no wings.

chrysalis
The third, pupal stage in the lives of butterflies and moths, during which the caterpillars are transformed into adults. Moth chrysalises are often enclosed in silken cocoons.

clutch
The number of eggs laid by a female at one time.

cocoon
(1) The shelter spun from silk thread by some insect larvae in which they turn into pupae.
(2) A silky covering or egg case made to protect a spider's eggs.

crocodilian
A member of the group of animals that includes crocodiles, alligators, gharials and caimans.

down
Fine, hairy feathers for warmth, not flight. Young chicks have only down and no flight feathers.

egg tooth
A small tooth that snakes and birds use to help them escape from the egg when they hatch.

equids
Horses and horse-like animals, such as asses and zebras.

fertilization
The joining together of a male sperm and a female egg to start a new life.

fledging/fledgling
The time when a bird starts to fly is called fledging. A fledgling is a young bird that has just reached this stage.

grooming
The way an animal cares for its coat and skin. It can be

carried out by the animal itself or by one animal for another.

habitat
The particular place where a group of animals lives.

hatchling
A young animal that has recently emerged from its egg.

herd
A group of animals that remain together. Elephant herds are made up of several family units, together with adult bulls. A large herd may have 1,000 individual elephants. Herds of horses are animals which travel together, usually consisting of a stallion, several mares and their foals.

incubation
Keeping eggs warm so that development can take place.

insect
One of a group of invertebrate animals (ones with no backbone). An insect has three body parts, six legs and usually one or two pairs of wings.

instinct
A behavior that an animal can carry out from a very early stage without having to learn how to do it. All members of a species have the same instincts.

juvenile
A young animal. In birds, juveniles have not grown their adult plumage.

labor
To give birth.

lagoon
A shallow, sheltered part of the sea, close to land.

larva (plural: larvae)
The young of insects that undergo complete metamorphosis, such as beetles and butterflies. Larvae are also called grubs, caterpillars or maggots.

Latin name
The scientific name for a species. An animal often has many different common names. For example, the bird called an osprey in Europe is sometimes referred to as a fish hawk in North America. The Latin name prevents confusion because it never alters.

life cycle
A series of stages in the life of an animal as it grows up and becomes an adult.

litter
The number of babies a mother gives birth to at one time.

mammal
One of a group of animals with a bony skeleton. Mammals feed their young on milk.

mare
Adult female horse.

mature
Developed enough to be capable of reproduction.

membrane
A thin skin or layer.

metamorphosis
The transformation of a young insect into an adult. Beetles and butterflies have four stages in their life cycle: egg, larva, pupa and adult. This is called complete metamorphosis.

milk teeth
The teeth of a young mammal that are replaced by adult teeth later.

molting
(1) When a young, growing insect, spider or snake sheds its skin and grows a new, larger one.
(2) When a bird loses its feathers and grows new ones.

nectar
The sweet juice made by flowers that is the main food for adult butterflies and moths and many other insects.

nutrients
The goodness in foods that is essential for life.

placenta
The end of the umbilical cord, attached to the womb, through which an unborn mammal receives nutrients from its mother.

playfight
The games that young animals play to sharpen skills that will be used in later life.

plumage
The covering of feathers on a bird's body.

pod
A group of animals. In crocodilians, this refers to newly hatched animals. In whales and dolphins, a pod is a group which hunt together.

predator
An animal that hunts and kills other animals for food.

prey
An animal that is hunted by other animals for food.

pupa (plural: pupae)
The third stage in the life of many insects, between the larval stage and the adult.

raptor
Any bird of prey. From the Latin word *rapere* meaning to seize, grasp or take by force.

regurgitate
To bring up food that has already been swallowed.

reptile
A group of scaly, cold-blooded animals, including crocodilians and snakes. Reptiles usually hatch from eggs.

scrape
A patch of ground cleared by a bird to lay its eggs on.

social animal
An animal that lives with others of its species in a cooperative group.

spiderling
A young spider that looks more or less like the fully-grown adult, but is smaller.

spinneret
The organ of a spider or a caterpillar through which silk emerges.

stallion
Adult male horse.

suckle
To feed a baby animal on milk from its mother's body.

territory
An area that an animal uses for feeding or breeding. Animals will defend their territory against others of their species.

umbilical cord
The cord running between an unborn baby mammal and its mother, through which it receives nutrients.

weaning
The change as a young animal gradually stops drinking its mother's milk and starts eating solid food.

yolk
Food material that is rich in protein and fats. It nourishes a developing embryo inside an egg.

Index